# Christmas Scroll Saw

# Ornament Designs

## Michelle Lyons

ISBN: 978-0-692-49595-7

Published in 2015 by Lignum Press
www.lignumpress.com

# Table of Contents

# About the Author

Michelle was born and raised in Southern Maryland. As a child, she learned to cross stitch and crochet from her mother and Nana, and began to develop a love for creating handmade gifts. After graduating from college, she began making Christmas ornaments from pre-packaged kits, and eventually began to look for something more challenging. Shortly thereafter, she purchased a scroll saw and has been covering her garage with sawdust ever since. Michelle currently resides in Maryland, where she enjoys playing volleyball, hiking, and creating beautiful Christmas ornaments to share with friends and family.

# Acknowledgements

I'd like to take this opportunity to thank several people who have contributed to the creation of this book. First, I extend a tremendous thank you to Tim for teaching me to strive for excellence in all pursuits and also for providing his insightful artistic expertise. I'd also like to thank my Aunt Tina for repeatedly encouraging me to copyright my first designs, as that spurred me to create the larger collection that is presented in this book. Thank you to Burkey and Melvin, who provided a very helpful second and third pair of eyes. And lastly, thank you to my parents, Renee, Diana, and all others who have given me such wonderful feedback on the finished ornaments!

# Introduction

# Motivation

I've always enjoyed crafting and making gifts for family and friends. Many years ago I started making Christmas ornaments, usually from a crafting kit of some sort. But over time I started having trouble finding ornaments that were different from the ones I had already made.

In 2001, I was watching a crafting show on TV and happened to see someone demonstrating how to use a scroll saw. I thought it was intriguing and might work well for making ornaments, so I bought one to try out.

I started out by using patterns from magazines and books like this one. Everyone seemed to love the finished wooden ornaments, and eventually I decided to branch out and make my own patterns.

The first ornament I designed was the Ice Skates pattern (page 87). The design was inspired by a handmade ornament I had inherited from my Nana, where the boots were made from white felt stuffed with cotton, paper clips formed the blades, and the laces were fashioned from red embroidery floss.

For a few years I designed a new Christmas ornament each September, and then I cut out enough pieces to hand out over the holiday season. People started encouraging me to create more patterns, and I began to think about creating a set of designs large enough to fill a book.

At first I felt a little overwhelmed because up until this point, I was spending three or four weeks on a single ornament design. But one night, an image of a snowman with a flowing scarf popped into my head. I immediately got up and sketched it on a piece of paper. That spark inspired me to keep designing, and the results (including the Snowman pattern) are contained in the pages of this book.

# Tools

**Scroll Saw.** There are several types of scroll saws on the market today. I am currently using the same saw I purchased over 10 years ago, which is a 20" variable speed scroll saw. Because there is such a wide variety of saws and features available, you should spend some time reading reviews before making a purchase. The 20" table is more than large enough to handle the projects in this book, and I think the variable speed feature is very helpful when cutting out sections of varying complexity or when dealing with different types of wood.

**Figure 1. Variable speed scroll saw**

**Blades.** A large selection of blades is available for use with the scroll saw (skip tooth, reverse skip tooth, crown tooth, spiral, etc.). I find that the reverse skip tooth blades work best for the ornament projects in this book. I use size #2R for most of the cutouts, but when the area is small or has tighter turns, I use the smaller #2/0R blades. Ultimately, the brand, type, and size of blade you use will depend on your personal preference and skill level.

**Drill / Rotary Tool.** You will need a drill or rotary tool to create blade holes for interior cutout sections. The drill also comes in handy for quickly forming the small circular cutouts that appear in many of the patterns. A drill press helps to ensure that the drill remains steady and that the hole you create is straight, but it is not required. You can easily get by with a hand-held tool like the one shown in Figure 2. I typically use 1/32" and 3/64" drill bits for the blade holes. Other drill bit sizes up to ¼" are used for circular cut out sections.

**Wood Files.** Wood Files are not required, but I find they are sometimes helpful when trying to smooth rough edges of the interior section cut outs.

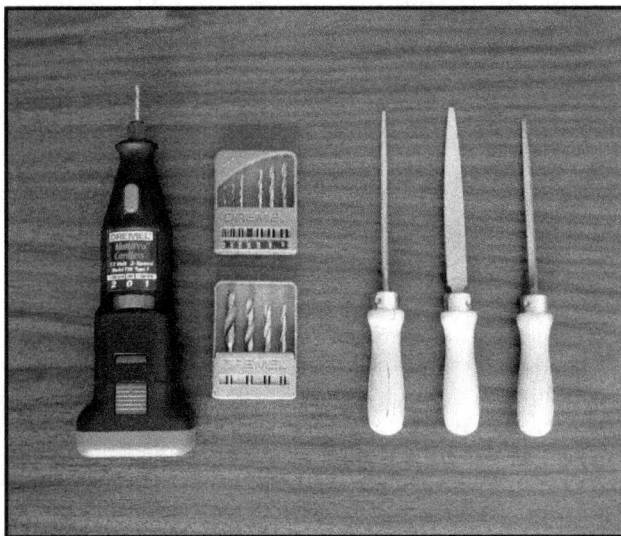

**Figure 2. Rotary tool and wood files**

**Safety Equipment.** It's a good idea to wear eye protection such as safety glasses while using the scroll saw. Also, drilling, sawing, and sanding can produce a fair amount of sawdust, so if you are sensitive to that you should also consider using a dust mask. Ear plugs or ear muffs will protect your ears against any loud noises generated by the saw or drill. Figure 3 shows examples of the safety equipment I use when making the ornaments in this book.

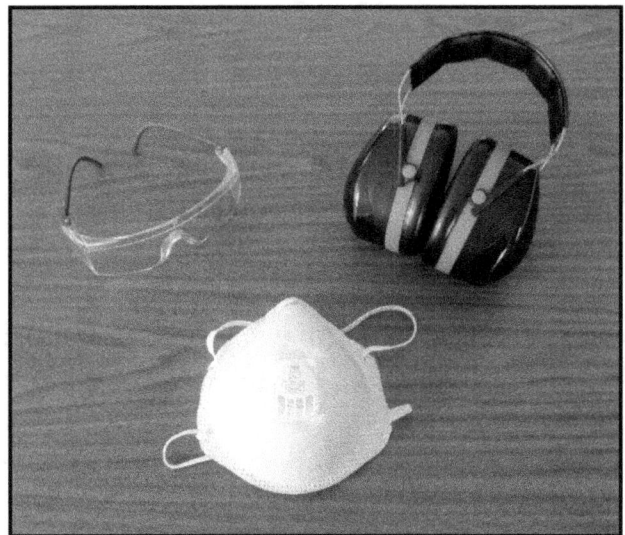

**Figure 3. Safety equipment**

# Materials

**Wood.** Many varieties of wood can be used for scroll saw projects (Baltic Birch plywood, Red Oak, Poplar, Aspen, etc.). Choose a grain and thickness that appeal to you. For the ornament projects in this book, I generally use ¼" thick Poplar, Aspen, or Basswood. You can find wood suitable for scroll sawing at hardware stores and woodworking shops, or you can order from stores online.

**Tape / Nails.** If you are going to cut out multiple ornaments at one time by stacking wood pieces, you will need some way to attach the pieces of wood together. I use blue painter's tape for this (see Figure 6). If you are stacking two pieces of wood that are ¼" thick, the 1" wide tape is a good choice. Another option is to attach the pieces of wood to each other using nails or brads.

**Patterns, Spray Adhesive, &Mineral Spirits.** The patterns you use will typically be printed on regular printer or photocopier paper. In order to attach the pattern to the wood, a spray adhesive such as Aleene's Respositionable Tacky Spray™ or 3M Super 77 Spray Adhesive™ will be required. After cutting out the ornament, you will be able to peel some or all of the pattern from the wood. Mineral spirits will help remove any remaining paper and adhesive residue.

**Sandpaper& Tack Cloth.** I normally use 150 or 180 grit sandpaper to smooth the surface and edges of the ornament after it is cut out. Loose sheets, sanding pads, or sanding blocks can all be used effectively. If you are going to leave the ornament unfinished, you can try higher grit sandpaper (220 or 320) for a smoother finish. A tack cloth will help remove any dust particles from the ornament.

**Finishes.** Typical finishes include varnish, wood stain, and paint. If you are happy with the natural color and grain pattern of the wood, then a simple varnish would be a good choice. If you like the grain but want to enhance the color, you can use wood stain. If you prefer a brighter, more colorful finish, or if the wood

surface is marred in some way and you want to cover it up, you can choose from a wide variety of paints. If you choose to stain or paint the ornament and you prefer a more polished appearance, you can also apply one or more coats of varnish over the stain or paint.

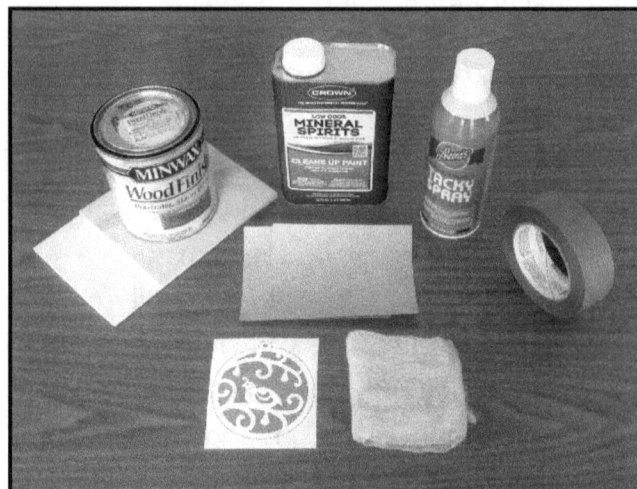

Figure 4. Materials

# Process

**Choose a pattern.** Browse through the pages of this book and choose a pattern. Make a copy of the pattern using a photocopier or scanner. Photocopiers and image software will allow you to enlarge or shrink the pattern to suit your needs. I like to size my ornaments in the 4" to 5" range when possible. For the most part, the patterns in this book are printed at the size I would use to create the ornament.

If you are just learning how to use the scroll saw, you can make any of the patterns simpler by ignoring one or more of the cutouts. An example of this is shown with the two Rocking Horse patterns on page 59.

**Prepare wood blanks.** Decide how you are going to orient your pattern on the wood. I usually like to have the grain oriented horizontally, but sometimes a pattern will look nicer with the grain oriented vertically. For example, compare the photos of the two book ornaments in Figure 5.

**Figure 5. Selecting an orientation**

In the top photo, the grain is oriented vertically, and in the bottom photo the grain is oriented horizontally. For this ornament, I prefer the appearance of the vertical grain in the top photo. This decision is a matter of personal preference, and each ornament pattern should be evaluated separately.

Once you choose an orientation, lay the pattern on the wood and make sure you have ½" or more on all sides. If your piece of wood is larger than needed, you can cut it to a workable size.

I like to stack two pieces of ¼" thick wood when cutting out these ornaments. Some people use nails or brads to attach the pieces of wood together, but I have had very good results using painter's tape. I simply tape two opposing sides, as shown in Figure 6. If you choose to use nails or brads, be sure that they do not protrude beyond the backside of the wood, as they will scratch the scroll saw table.

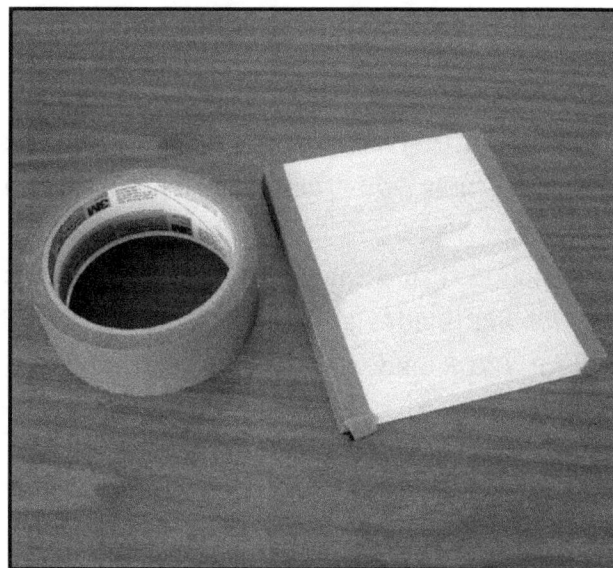

**Figure 6. Two boards taped together**

**Apply pattern to wood blanks**. Use a spray adhesive on the back of the pattern and apply the pattern to the wood blank. Press down over the entire pattern to make sure the paper adheres to the wood, as shown in Figure 7.

**Figure 7. Pattern adhered to wood**

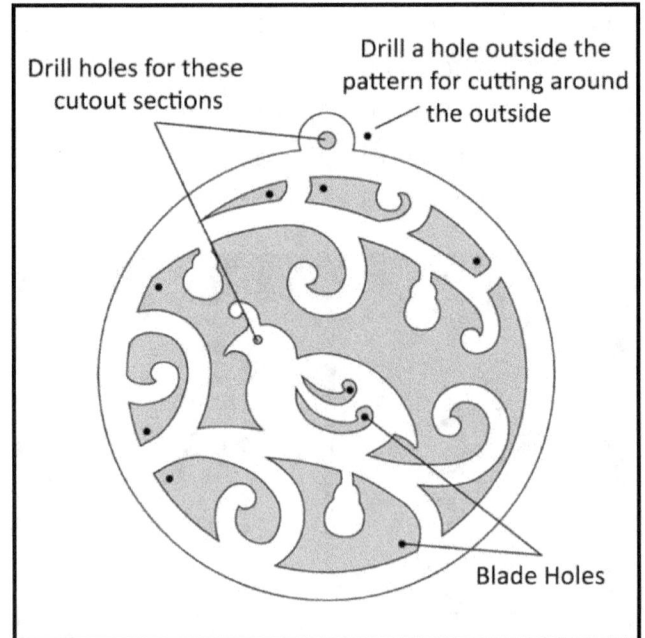

**Figure 8. Drill hole diagram**

**Drill holes in wood blanks**. Drill a hole in each gray section that appears on the pattern. The size of the hole you create will depend on the size of the blade you intend to use to cut out that section. I find that a 3/64" drill bit works well for #2R blades and a 1/32" drill bit works well for #2/0R blades.

Next, drill a hole outside the pattern outline for cutting around the outside of the pattern.

Lastly, if there are small circular cutouts in the pattern, you can use a drill to create those cutouts, rather than cut them out using the scroll saw. Choose the drill bit size that most closely matches the size of the circular cutouts.

Figure 8 includes small black dots to indicate where to drill blade holes for the interior sections. It also shows that the Partridge eye and ornament hanger can be drilled rather than cut out with the scroll saw.

Figure 9 shows how the boards look after the holes are drilled.

**Figure 9. Blade holes and circular cutouts**

**Cut out the pattern**. A general rule of thumb for cutting out these ornaments is to start with the small and delicate sections, then continue cutting from the center of the pattern and work your way to the outside of the pattern. By starting with the delicate sections, you are less likely to have those sections break when you are cutting them out.

For each of the gray sections in the pattern, thread the saw blade through the hole for the section and cut it out. Finish by cutting around the outside of the pattern.

Figure 10 shows the order in which I would cut out the interior sections for the Partridge pattern. Plan to cut out the pattern once as a test so you can identify any tricky or fragile spots.

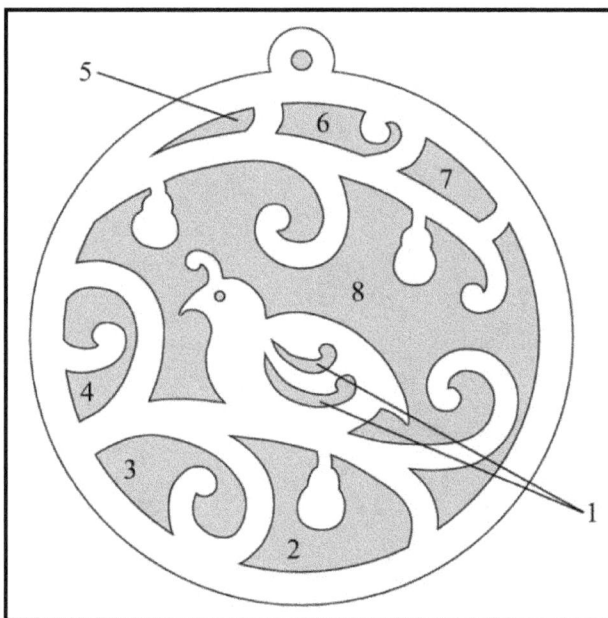

**Figure 10. Cutout order diagram**

**Remove pattern from wood**. Once you have finished cutting out the ornament you can remove the paper pattern from the wood. Depending on how well the adhesive is working, you may be able to peel the entire pattern off.

Other times, as shown in Figure 11, you might need to use mineral spirits to help remove the pattern from the wood. If the wood surface

feels sticky after the pattern is removed, wipe it with mineral spirits to remove the adhesive residue. Be sure to wait for the wood surface to dry out before moving to the next step.

**Figure 11. Remove pattern from wood**

**Sand the ornament**. Use sandpaper on the front and back surfaces and edges of the ornament. Make sure the wood surfaces feel smooth and there are no rough edges. If you have rough edges on interior cuts you can use wood files to help remove them. After sanding, wipe the surfaces of the ornament with the tack cloth to remove any dust particles.

**Apply a finish**. The sanded ornament can be painted, stained, varnished, or left unfinished. I recommend testing any finish on a scrap piece of wood before applying to an ornament.

I prefer the way the ornaments look when they are stained, and I typically leave them unvarnished. The ornaments pictured in this book were finished with Minwax™ Red Oak Wood Stain.

# Twelve Days of Christmas

Partridge

Turtle Doves

*French Hen*

*Calling Bird*

*Golden Rings*

*Goose a-Laying*

Swan a-Swimming

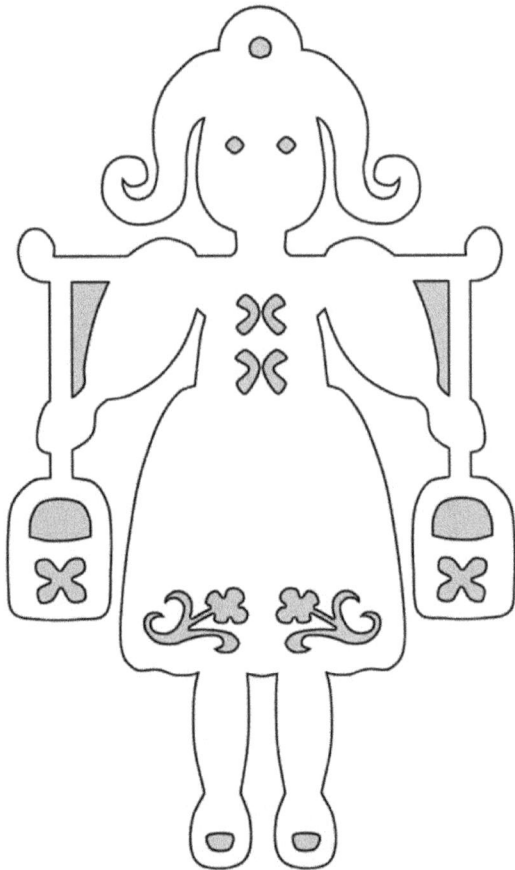

Maid a-Milking

Lady Dancing

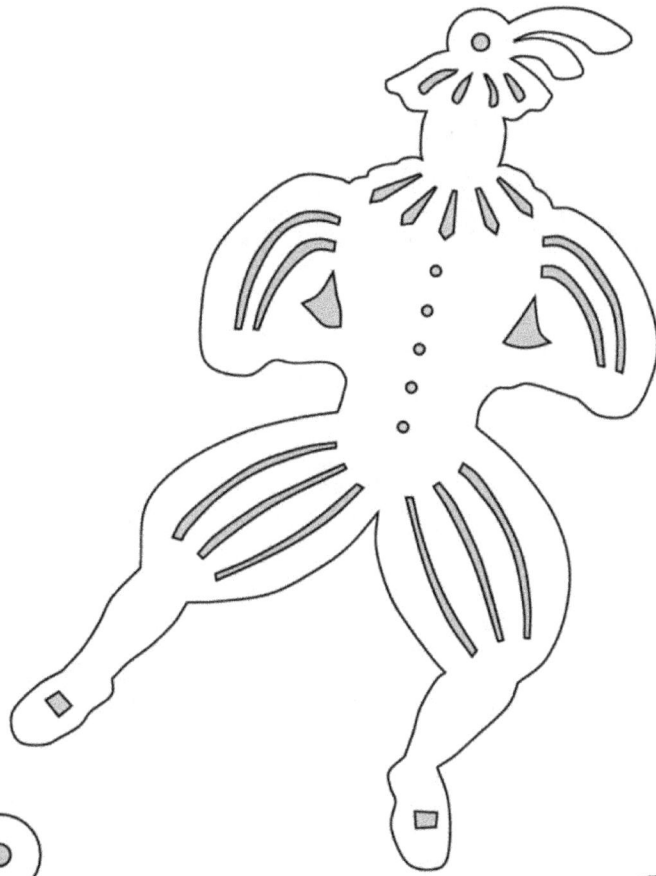

*Lord a-Leaping*

*Piper Piping*

*Drummer Drumming*

# Traditional

Ball Ornament Scroll

Ball Ornament Holly

Ball Ornament Star

*Bells Standard*

*Bells Snowflake*

*Bell Ornate*

*Bow*

*Calendar Plain*

*Calendar Holly*

*Candles*

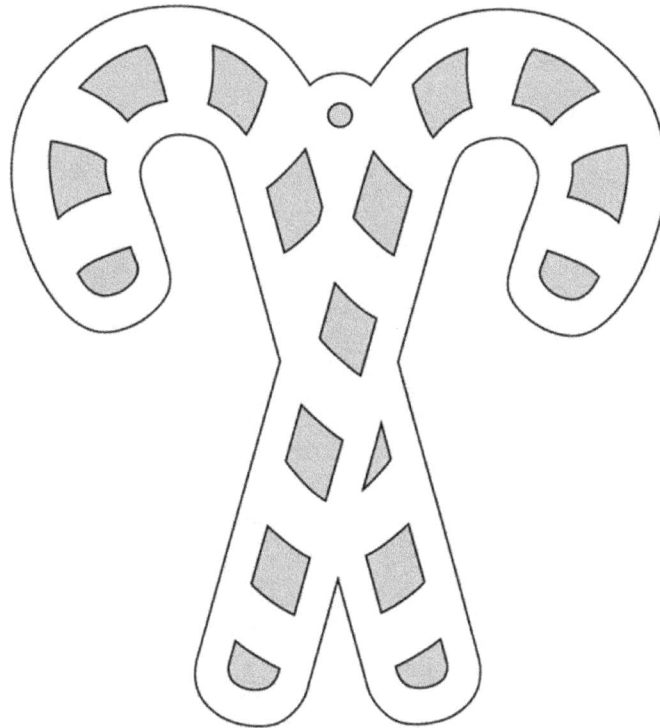

*Candy Canes Crossed*

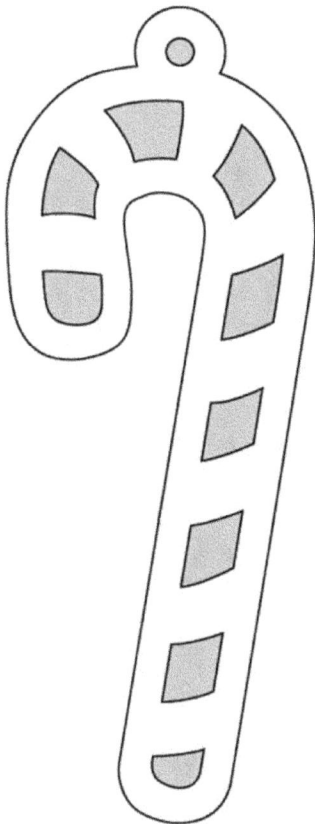

*Candy Cane*

*Candy Cane with Bow*

*Carolers*

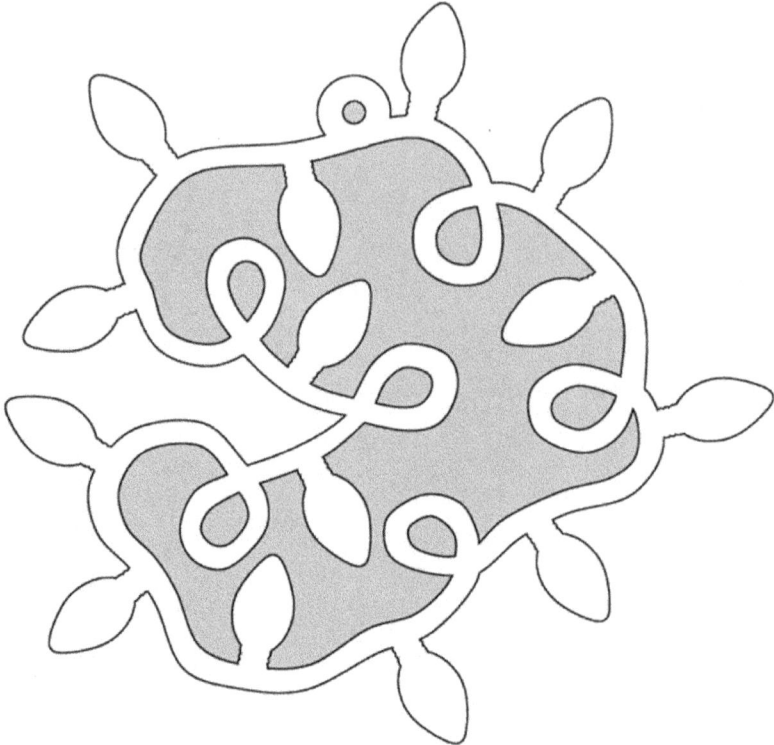

*Christmas Lights*

*Deer Head*

*Deer #1*

*Deer #2*

Elf #1

Elf #2

Elf #3

*Gingerbread House Flowers*

*Gingerbread House Hearts*

*Gingerbread Man*

*Gingerbread Woman*

*Holly*

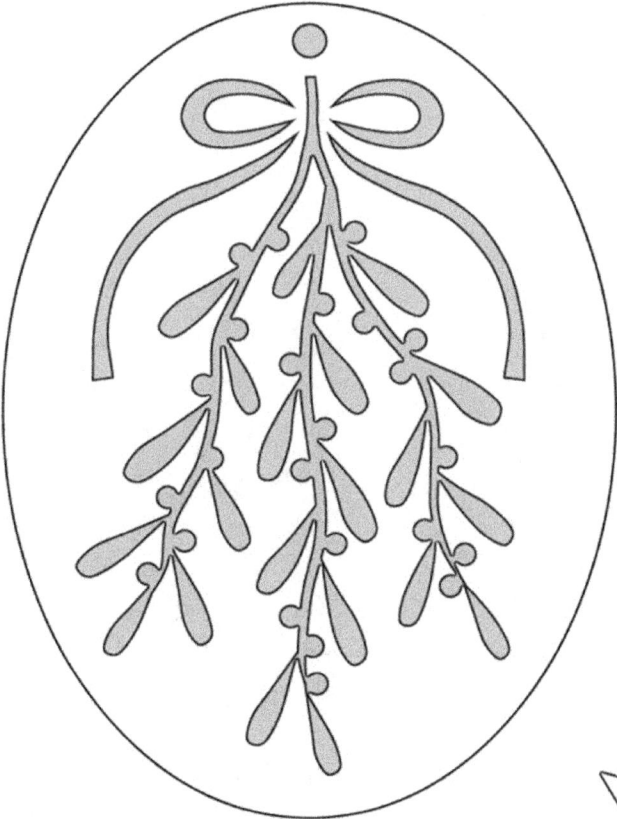

*Mistletoe*

*Poinsettia*

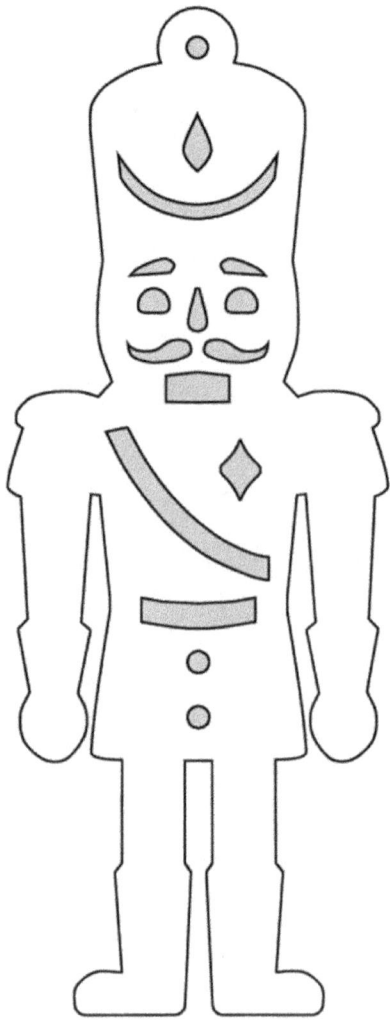

Nutcracker #1

Nutcracker #2

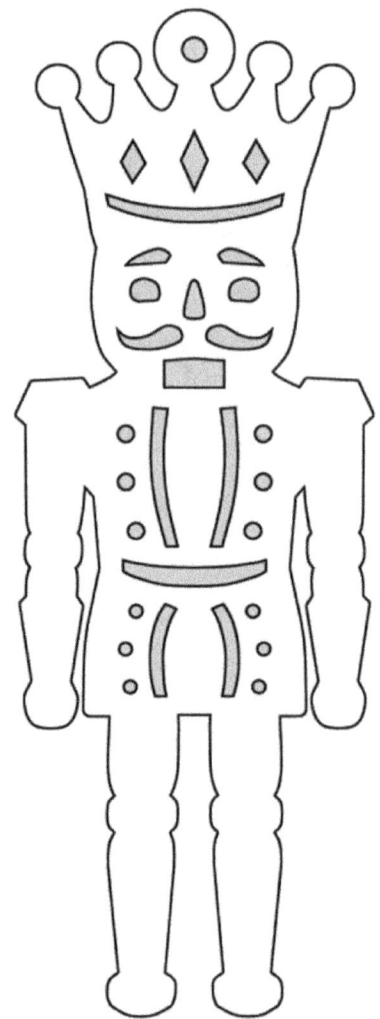

Nutcracker #3

*Present*

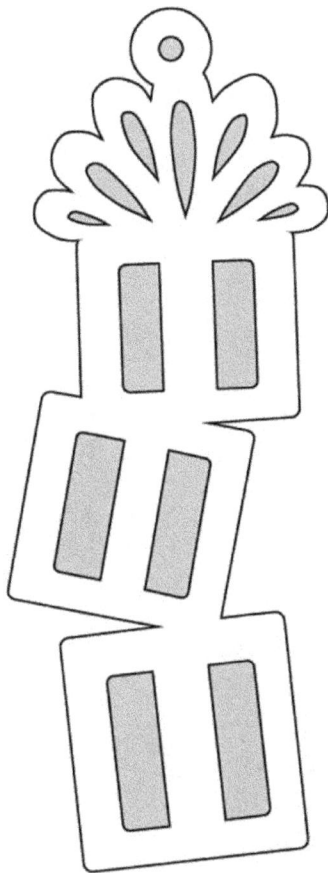

*Present Stack*

*Sack of Presents*

Santa with Pack

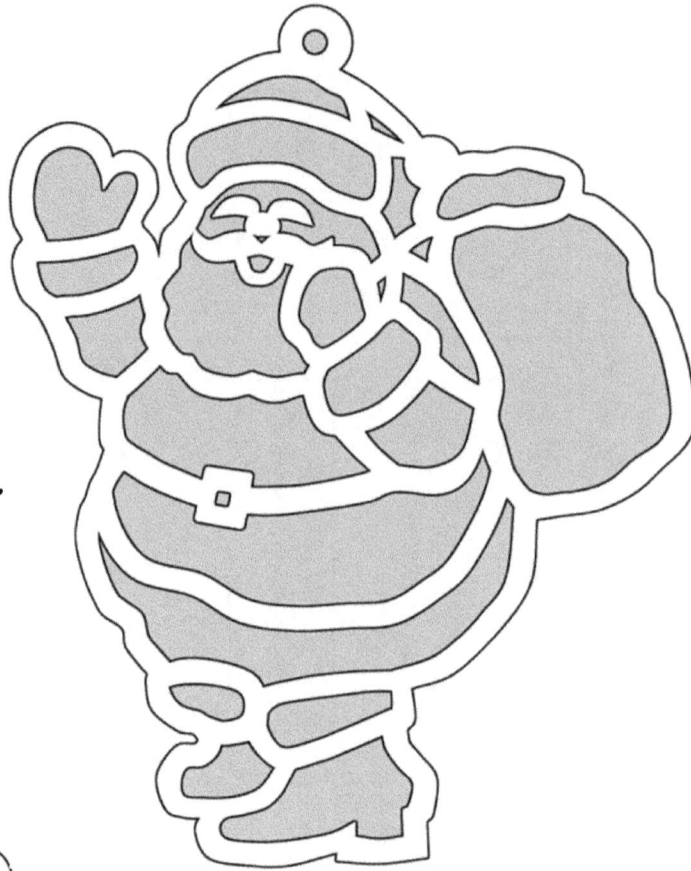

Santa Rooftop #1

Santa Rooftop #2

*Naughty List*

*Nice List*

*Star #1*

*Star #2*

*Stocking*

*Tree*

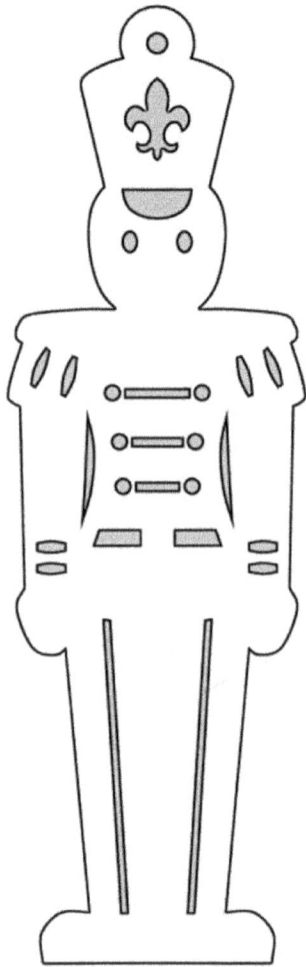

Toy Soldier #1

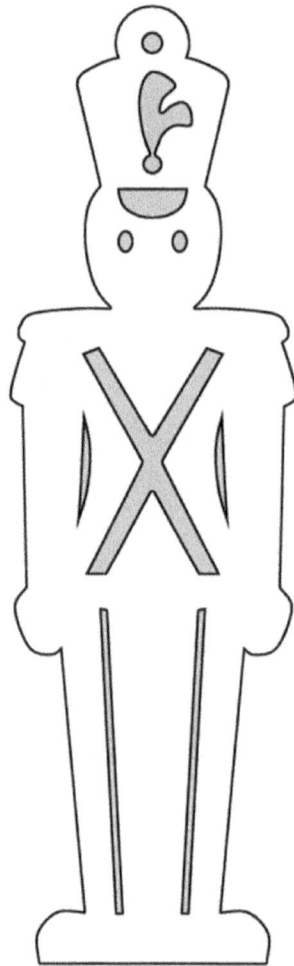

Toy Soldier #2

Toy Soldier #3

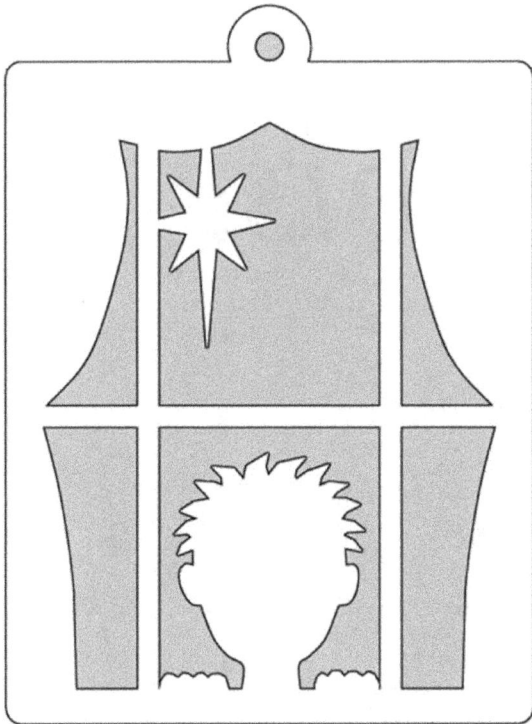

*Waiting For Santa Boy #1*

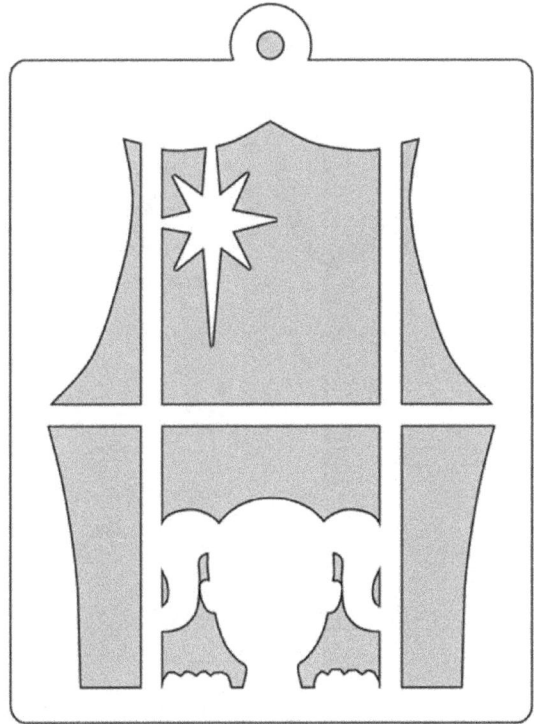

*Waiting For Santa Girl #1*

*Waiting For Santa Boy #2*

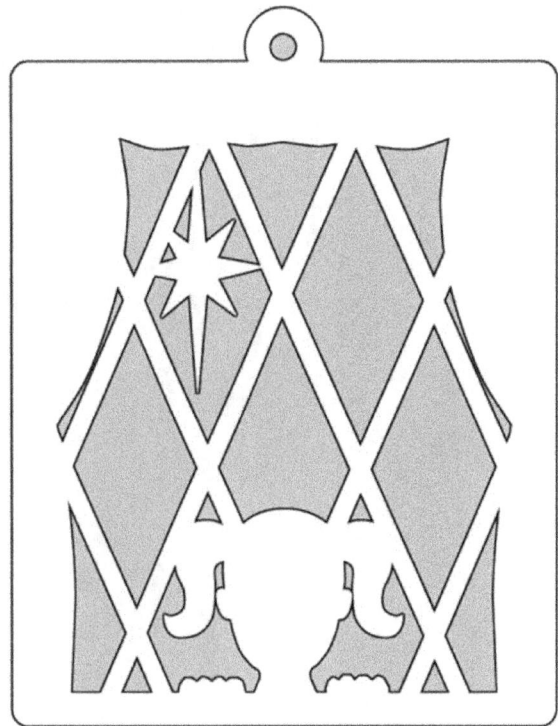

*Waiting For Santa Girl #2*

# Joyful Noise

Drum

Bass Clef

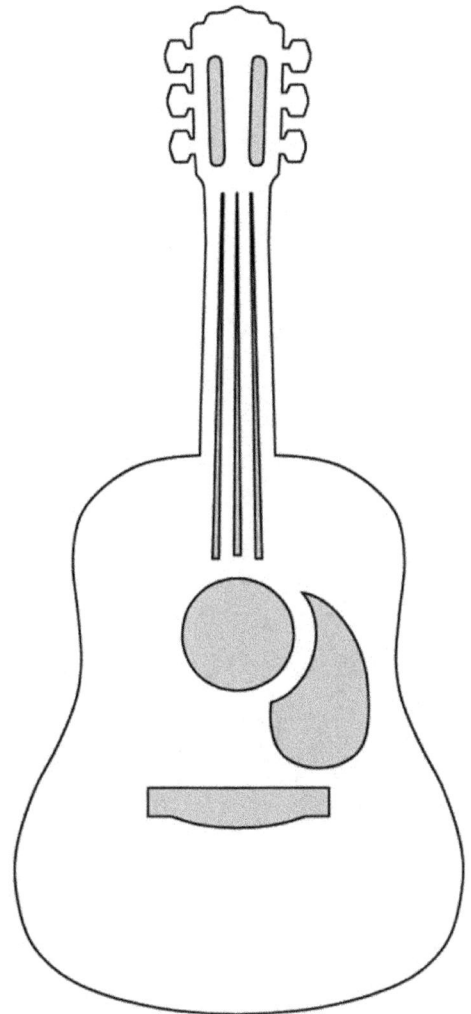

Guitar

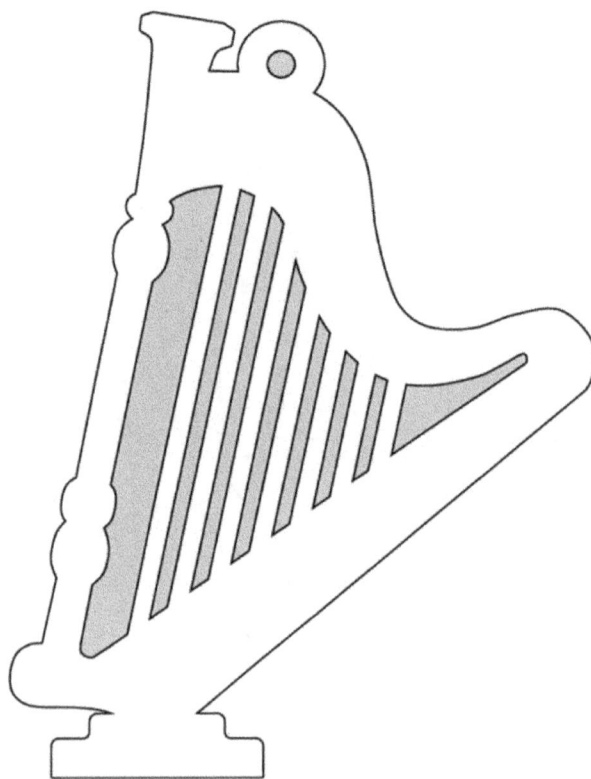

*Harp*

*Treble Clef*

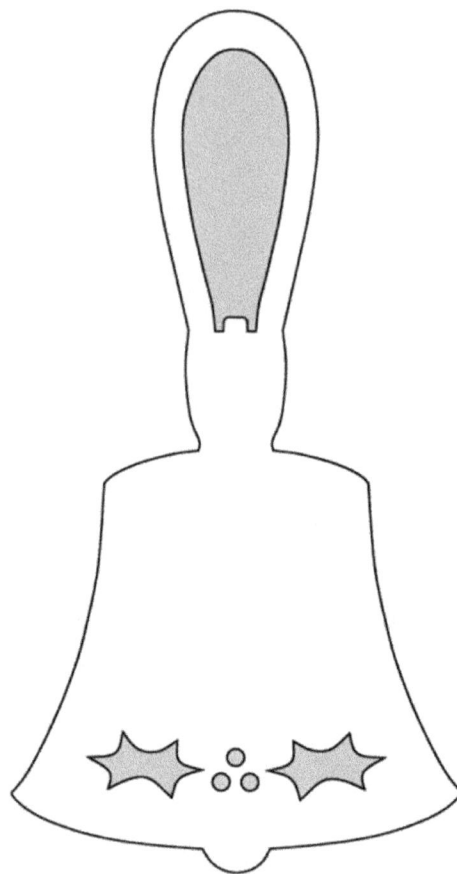

*Handbell*

*Horn with Bow*

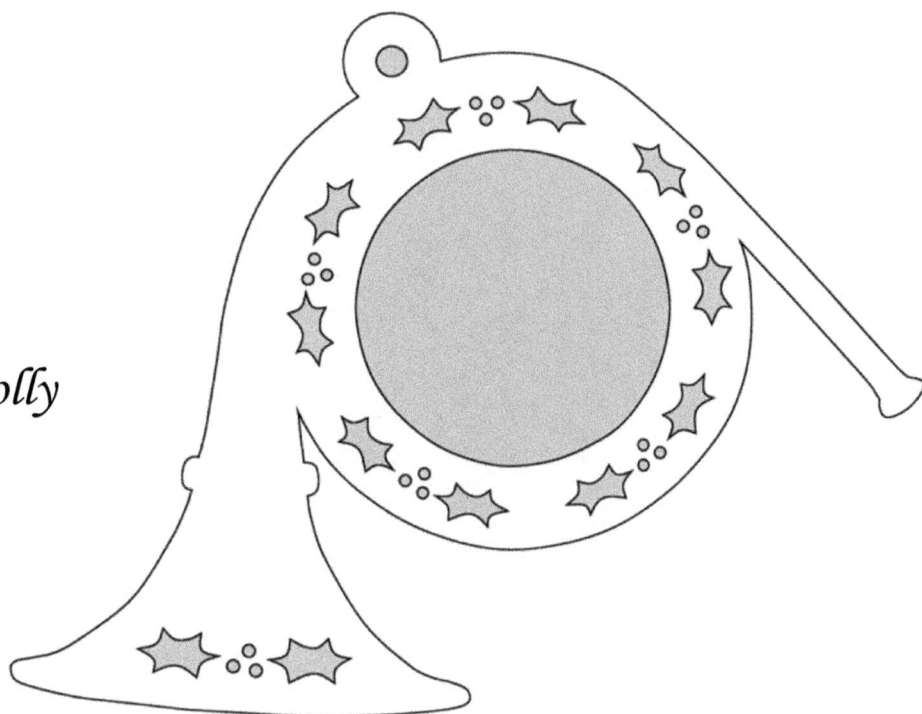

*Horn with Holly*

Violin

Sixteenth Notes

Piano

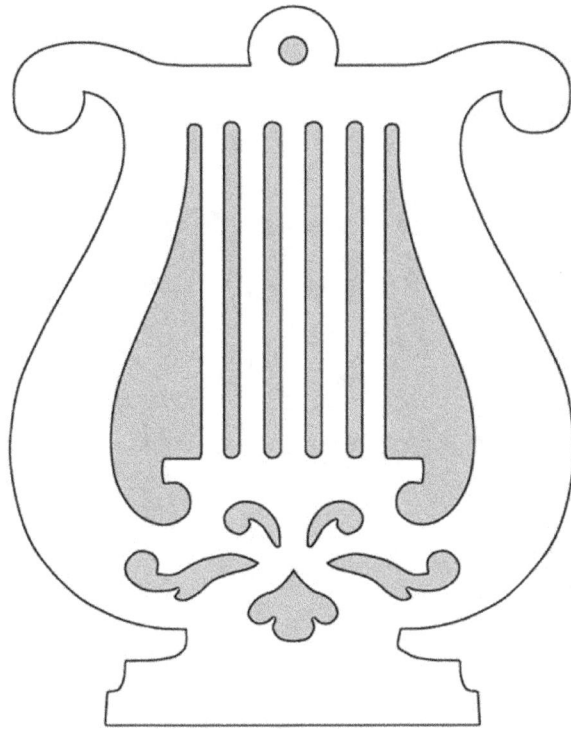

*Lyre*

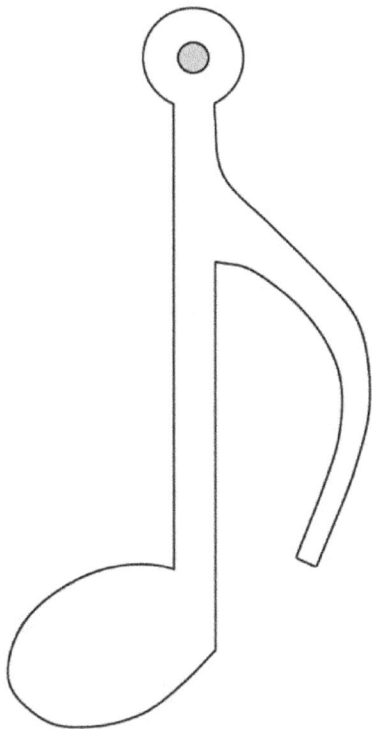

*Eighth Note*

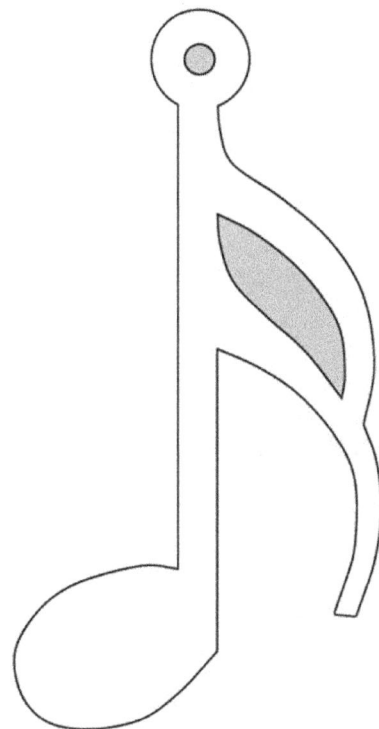

*Sixteenth Note*

*Away In A Manger*

*We Three Kings*

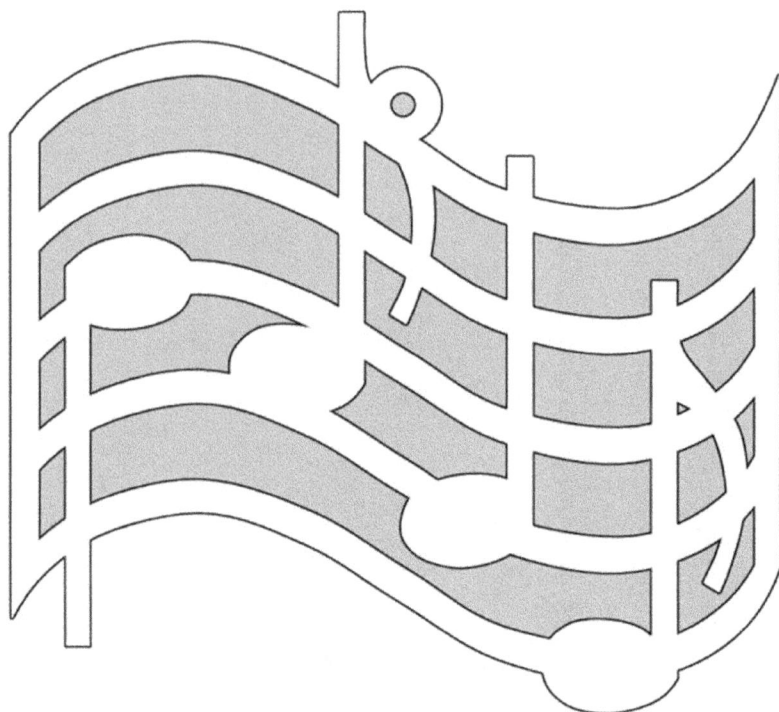

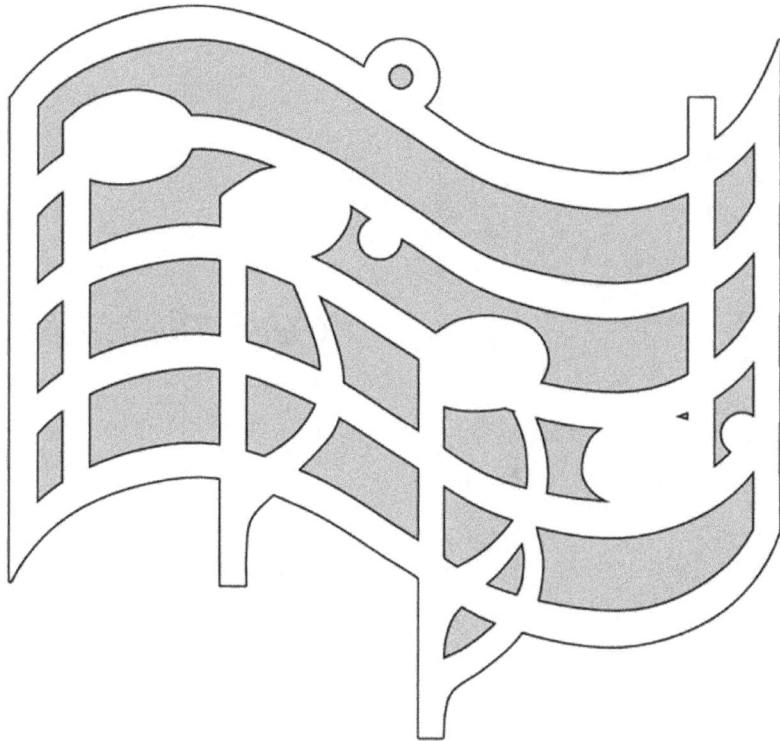

*Joy To The World*

*Hark The Herald*

*Angels Sing*

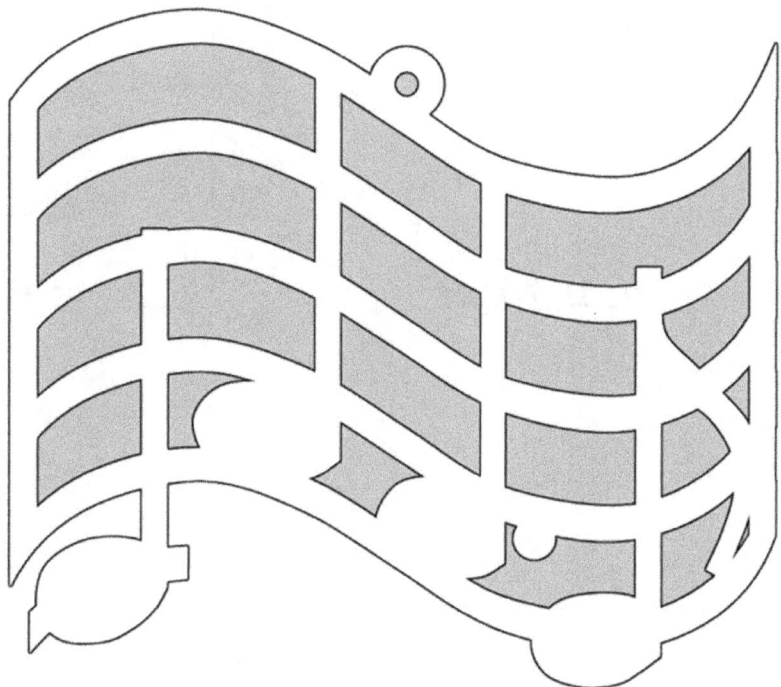

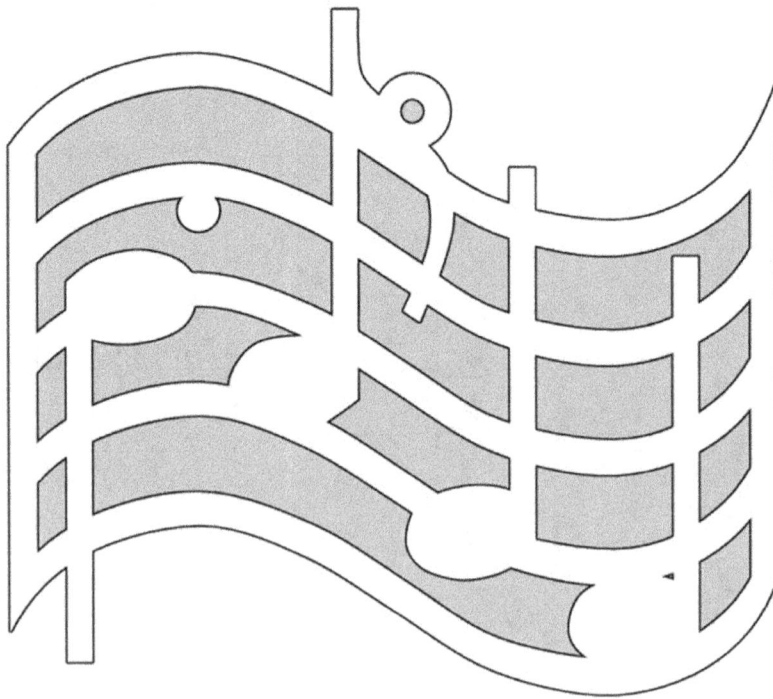

Deck The Halls

Silent Night

# *Religious*

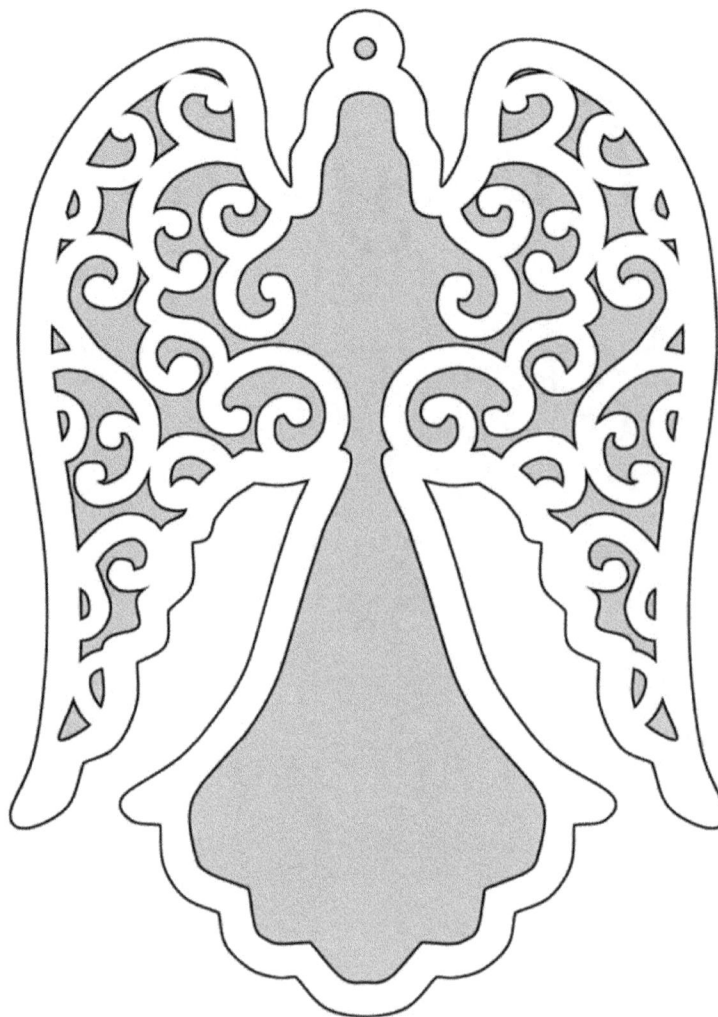

*Angel*

*ihs*

*Holy Bible*

*Luke 2:1-14*

*Choir Girl*

*Choir Boy*

*Church Window*

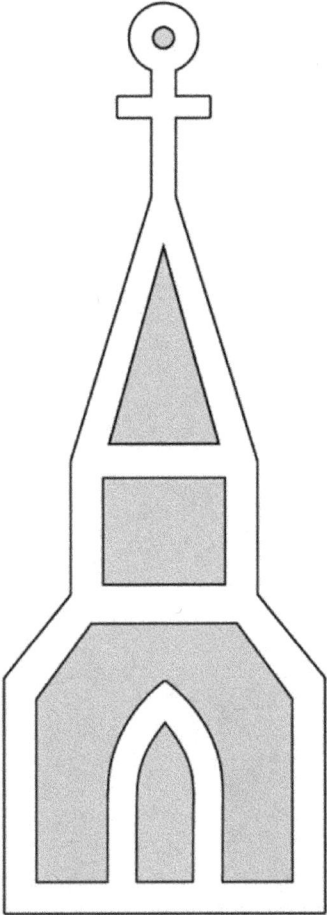

*Church #1*

*Church #2*

*Church #3*

Cross #1

Cross #2

Cross #3

Wiseman

Dove with Olive Branch

*Chi Rho*

*Cross #4*

*Manger*

*Journey to Bethlehem*

*Dove of Peace*

# Toys

Picture Book E-F

Picture Book S-T

Jack In The Box Diamond

Jack In The Box Star

Blocks

*Rocking Horse Simple*

*Rocking Horse Western*

Rag Doll Boy

Rag Doll Girl

Pull Duck

*Teddy Bear Heart*

*Teddy Bear Bow*

Baby Buggy

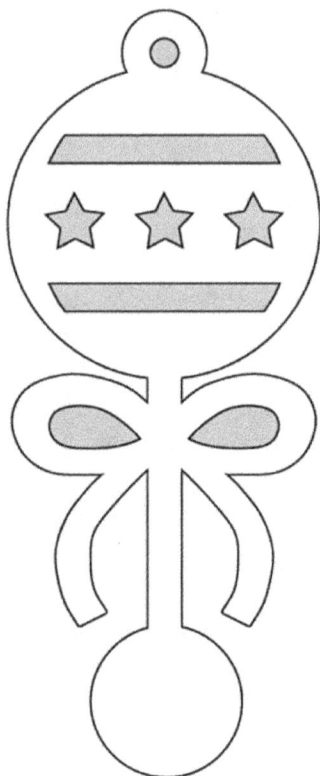 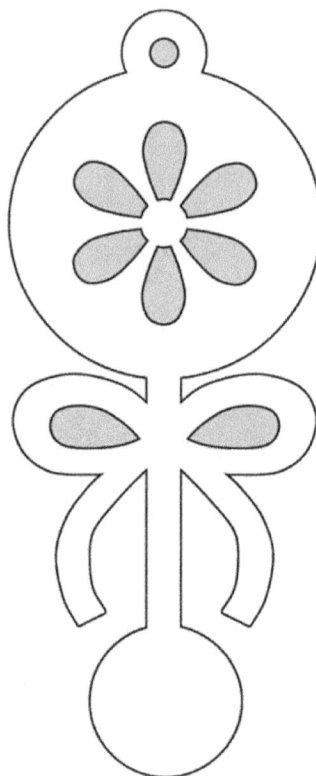 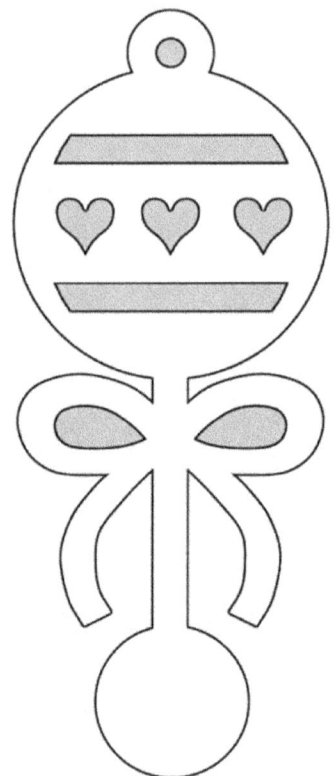

Rattles

*Tricycle Boy*

*Tricycle Girl*

*Soccer Ball*

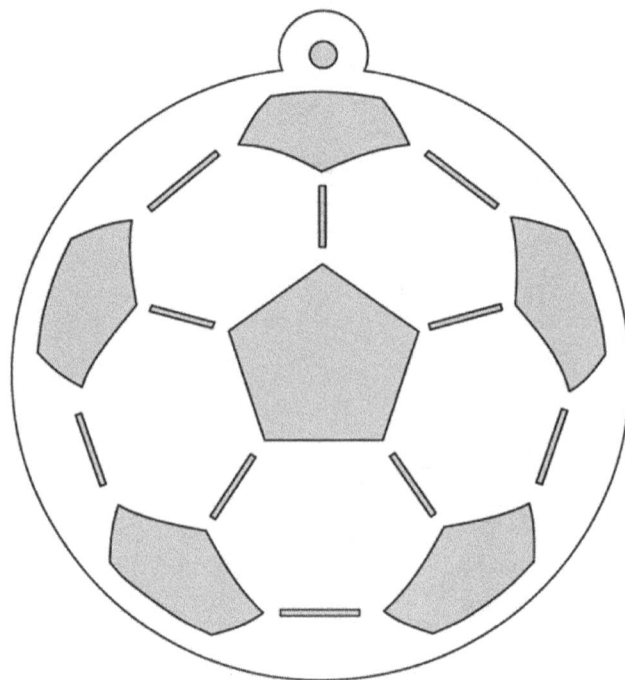

*Baseball*

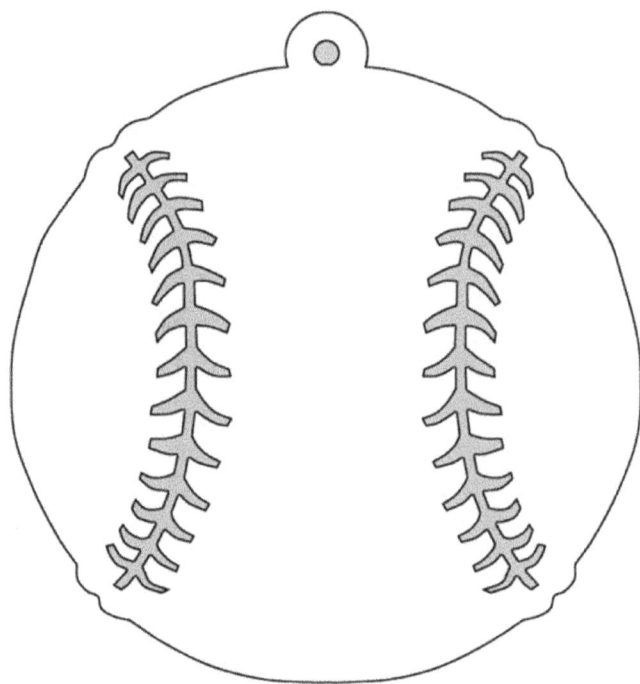

*Basketball*

Train Engine

Sail Boat

Football

*Five of Hearts*

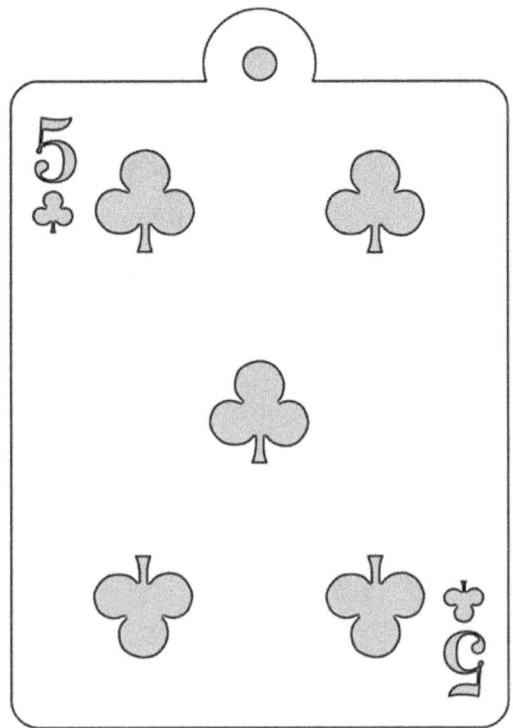

*Five of Clubs*

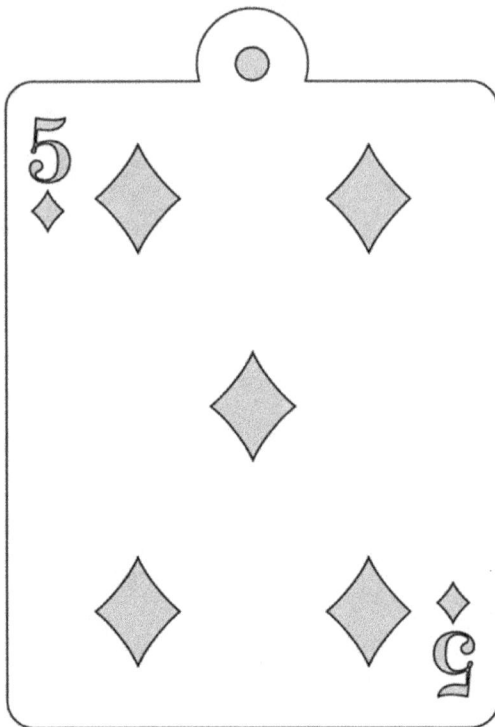

*Five of Diamonds*

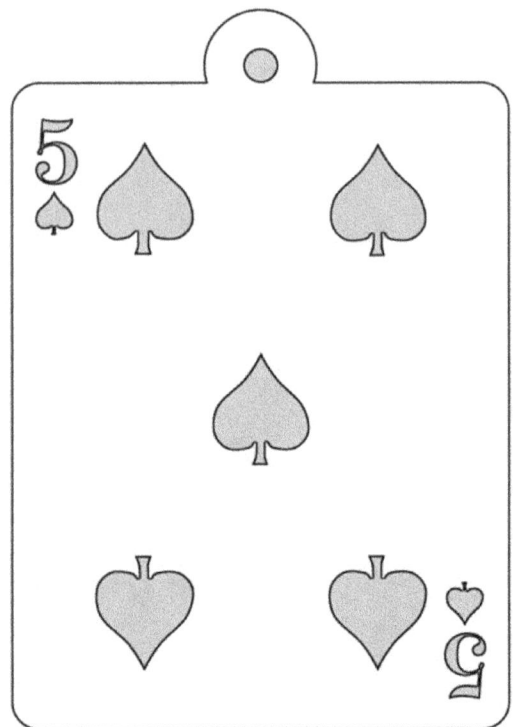

*Five of Spades*

# *Sentiments*

*Believe*

*Celebrate*

*Faith*

*Hope*

*Peace*

*Rejoice*

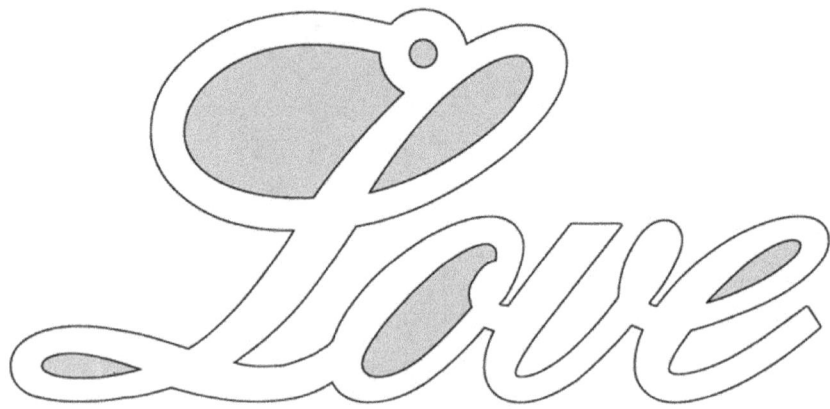

*Love*

*Family*

*Blessings*

*Deck The Halls*

*Good Will To Men*

*Buon Natale*

*Joyeux Noel*

*Feliz Navidad*

Happy Holidays

Happy New Year

Happy Hanukkah

Ho HoHo Holly

Ho HoHo Present

Little Drummer Boy

*Joy*

*Jesus*

*Jesus Christ*

*Let It Snow!*

*Make A Wish*

*Mary & Joseph*

*Merry Christmas*

*Mistletoe & Holly*

*Noel*

North Pole

O Holy Night

Peace On Earth

Saint Nicholas

_Silent Night_

_Think Snow_

*Star Of Bethlehem*

*Season's Greetings*

*Winter Wonderland*

# Winter

*Building A Snowman*

*Cardinal*

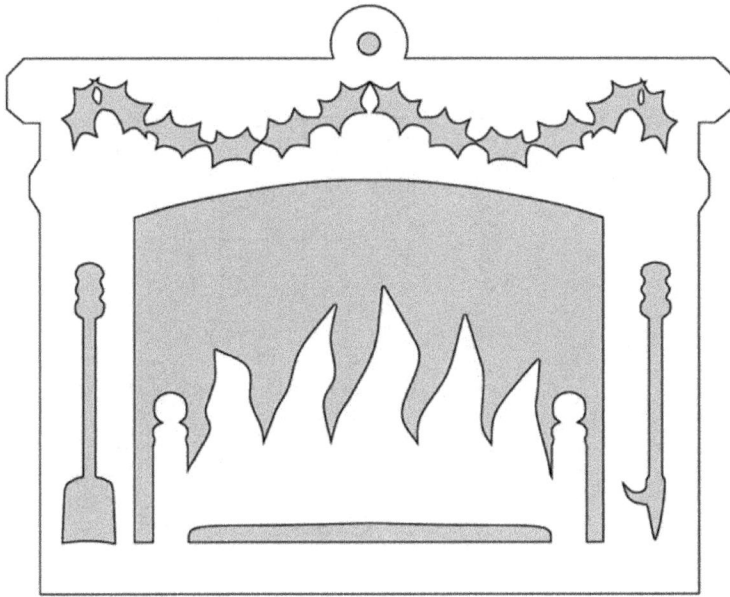

*Fireplace Garland*

*Skier*

*Fireplace Stockings*

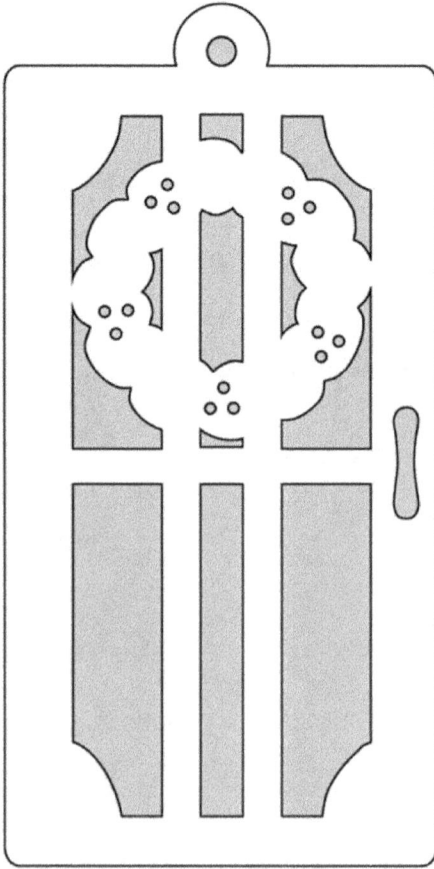

Front Door #1

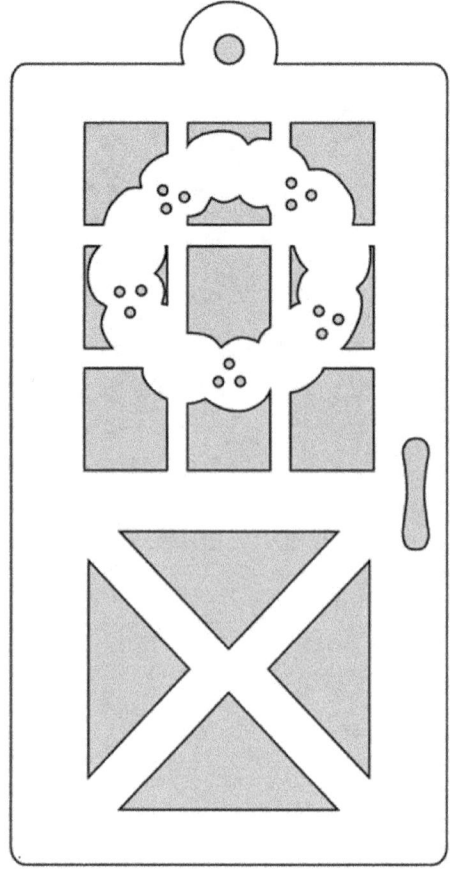

Front Door #2

Mailbox

*Ice Skates*

*Ice Skater*

Lantern

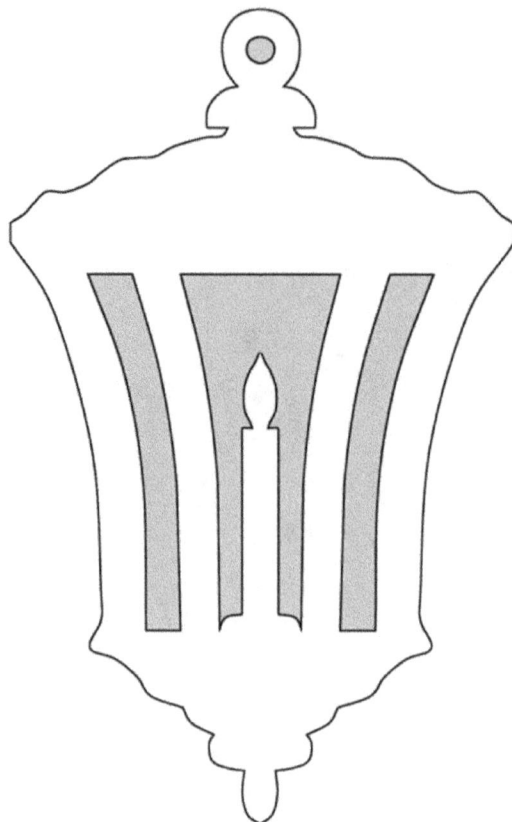

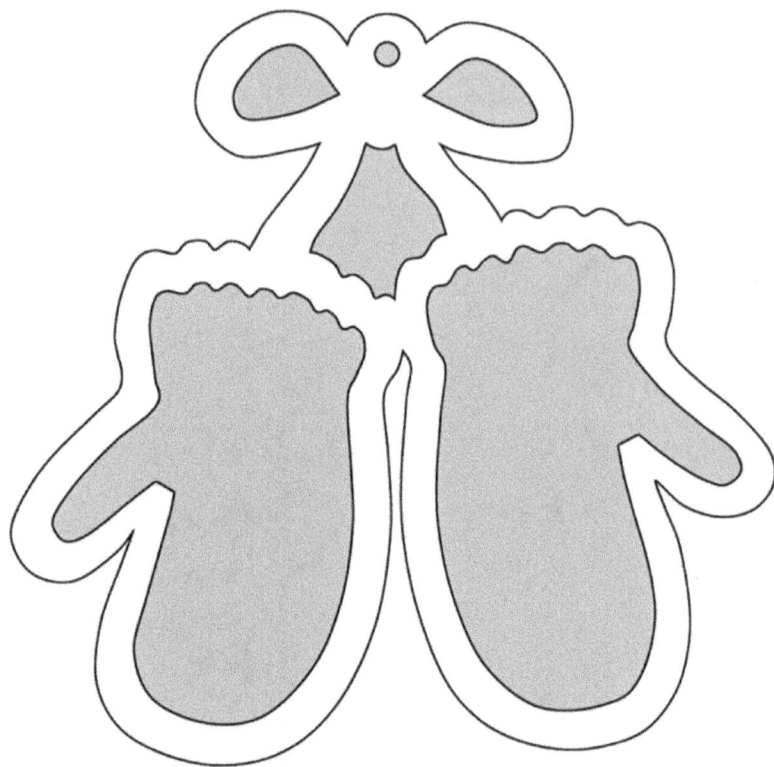

Mittens Outline

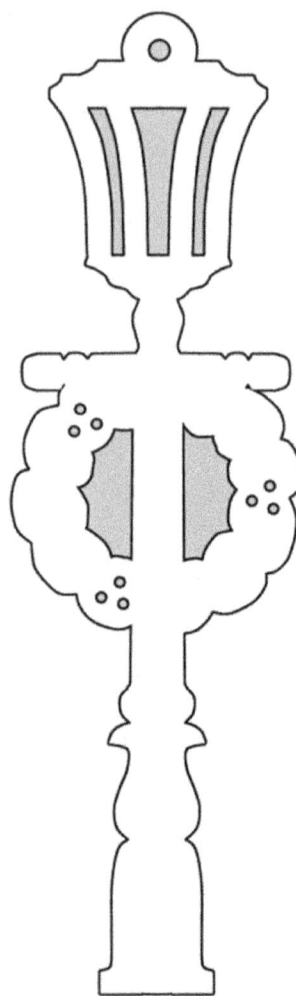

Lamp Post

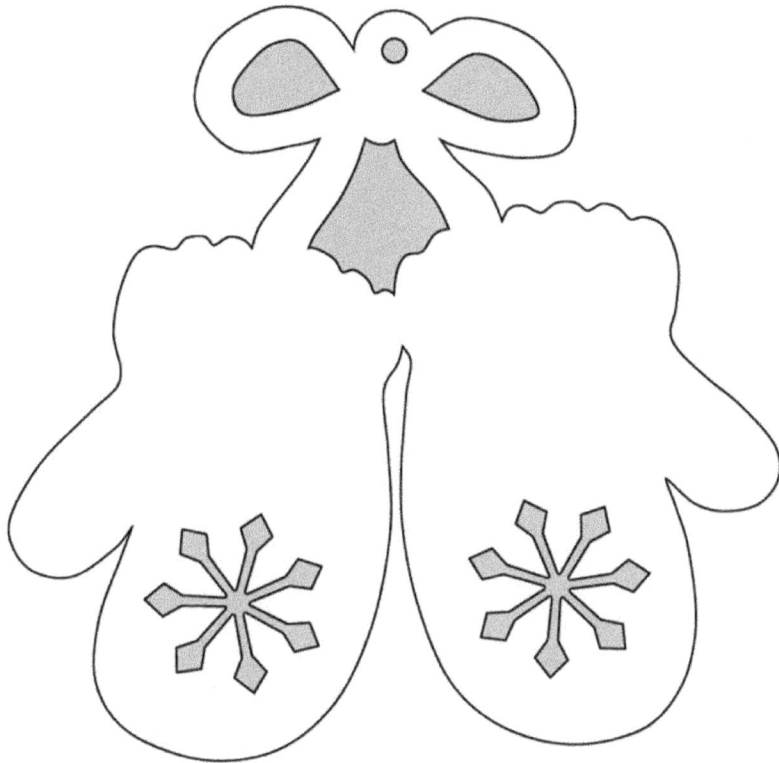

*Mittens Snowflake*

*Mittens Crisscross*

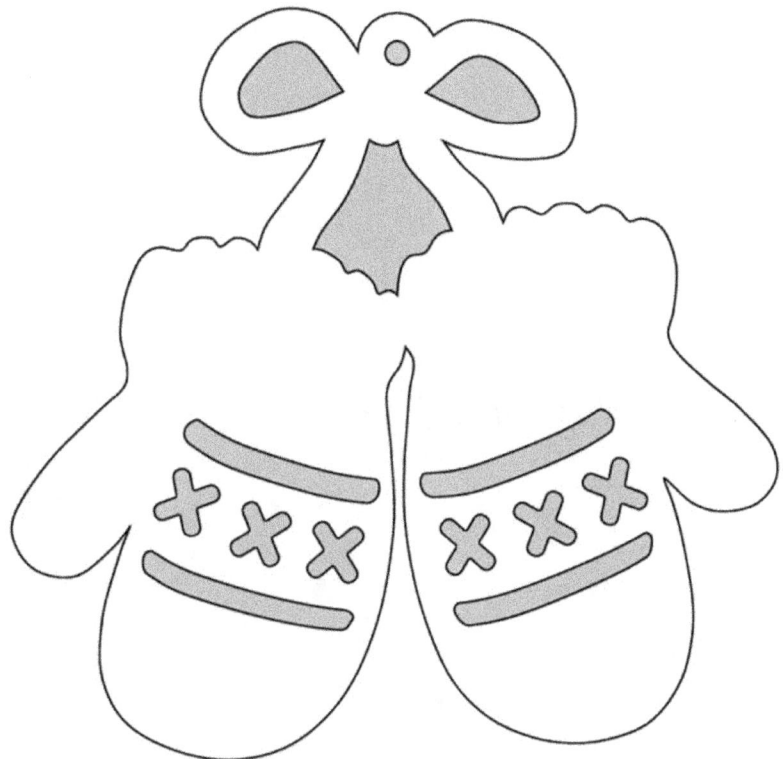

*Mug Holly*

*Mug Snowflake*

*Snowman*

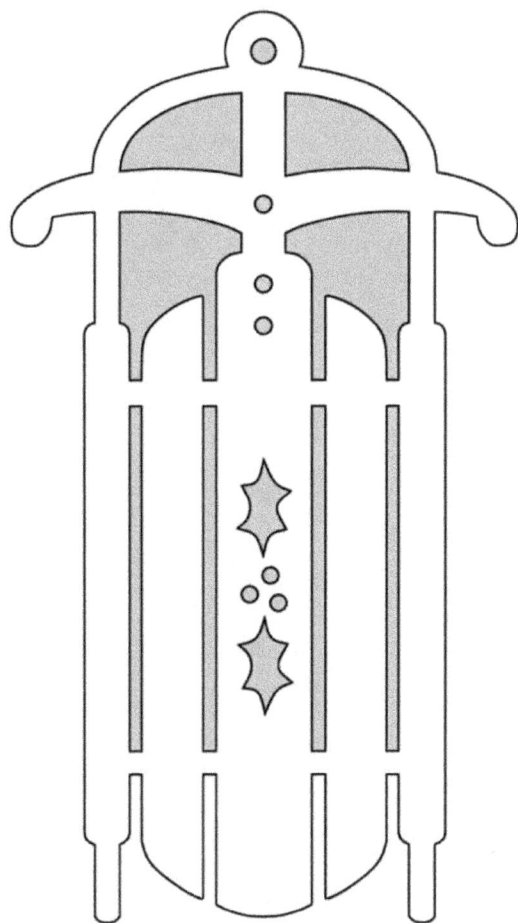

*Sled*

*Sleigh*

# Snowflakes

*Snowflake #1*

*Snowflake #2*

*Snowflake #3*

*Snowflake #4*

*Snowflake #5*

*Snowflake #6*

*Snowflake #7*

*Snowflake #8*

*Snowflake #9*

*Snowflake #10*

*Snowflake #11*

*Snowflake #12*

*Snowflake #13*

*Snowflake #14*

*Snowflake #15*

*Snowflake #16*

*Snowflake #17*

*Snowflake #18*

*Snowflake #19*

*Snowflake #20*

# Design Your Own

This section contains a set of simple pattern outlines from the book that you can customize for yourself.

All you have to do is make a copy of the pattern you want to modify, then draw your own cut-out sections in the interior of the ornament.

This technique can be used with any of the pattern outlines in this book. Simply trace the outline and fill the interior of the pattern with your own design.

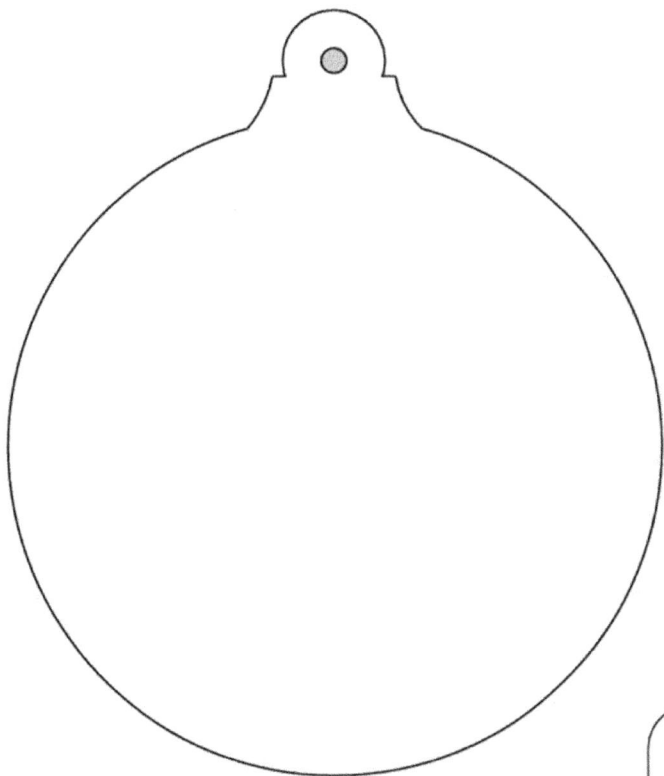

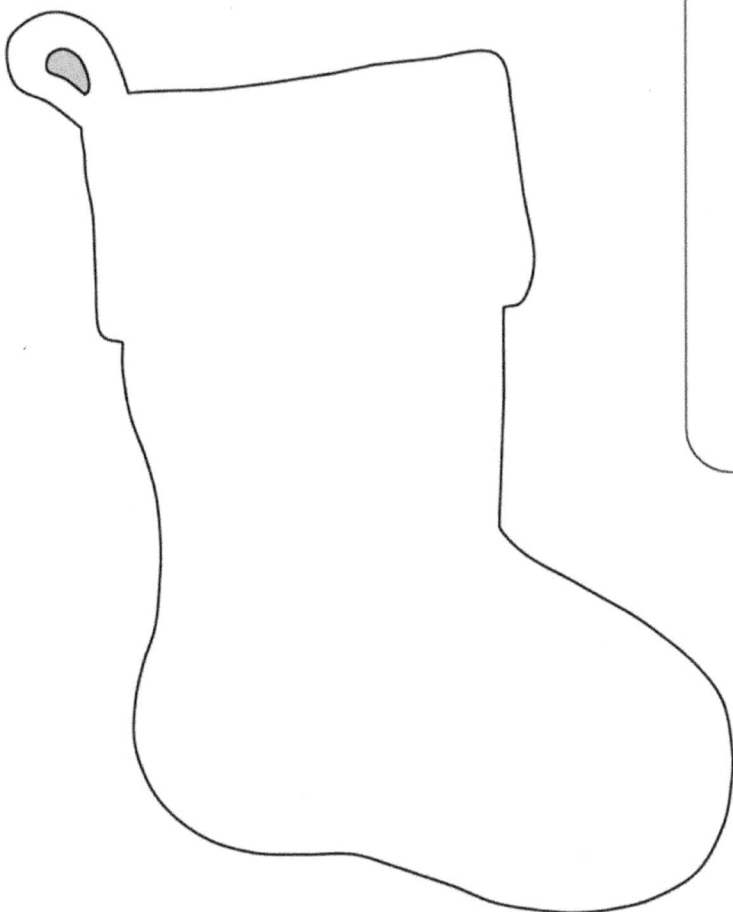

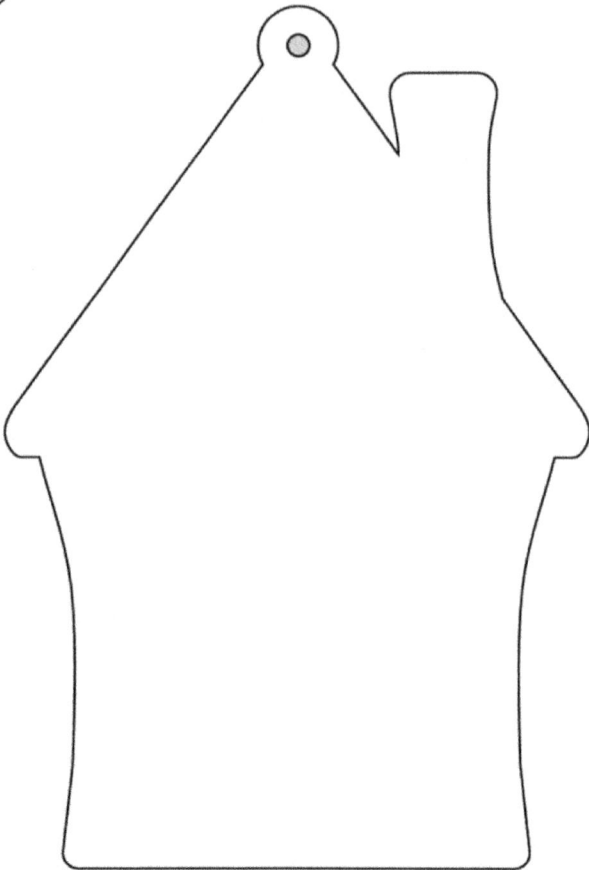

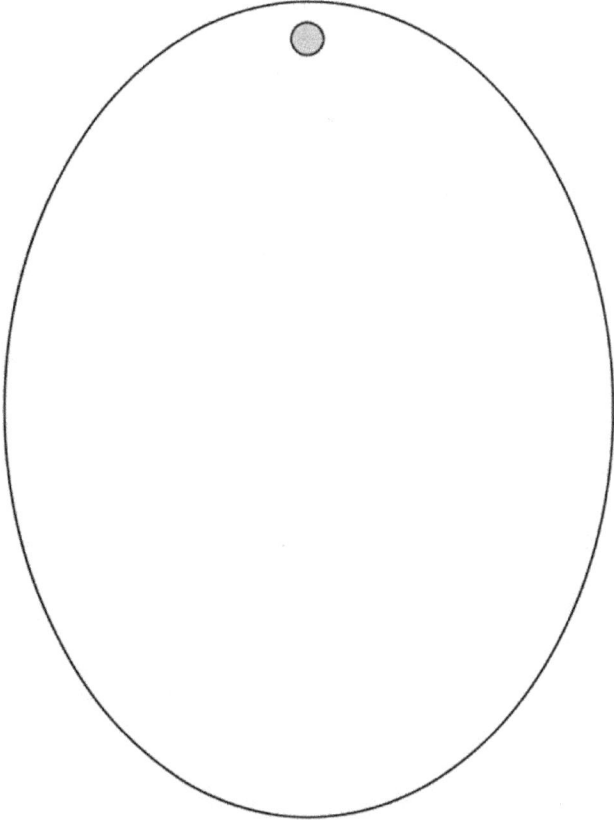

# Photo Gallery

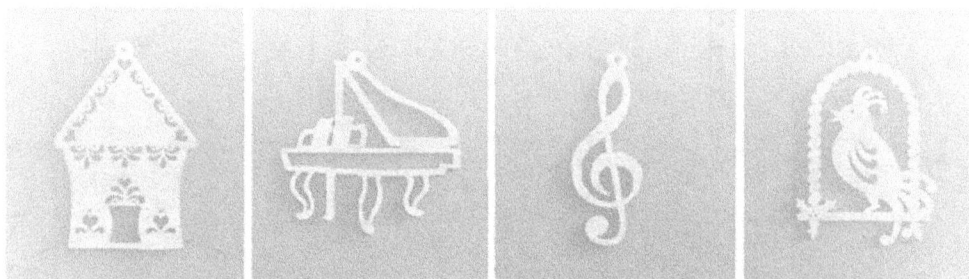

| | | | |
|---|---|---|---|
| Gingerbread House Flowers | Piano | Treble Clef | Calling Bird |

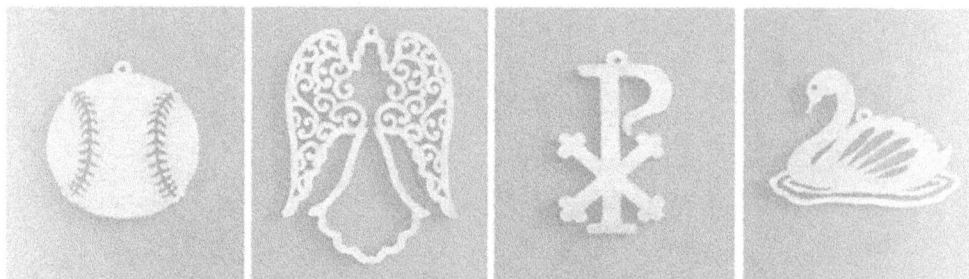

| | | | |
|---|---|---|---|
| Baseball | Angel | Chi Rho | Swan a-Swimming |

| | | | |
|---|---|---|---|
| Five of Clubs | Football | Ice Skater | Ice Skates |

*Partridge*

*Turtle Doves*

*French Hen*

*Calling Bird*

*Golden Rings*

*Goose a-Laying*

*Swan a-Swimming*

*Maid a-Milking*

*Lady Dancing*

Lord a-Leaping

Piper Piping

Drummer Drumming

Ball Ornament Holly

Ball Ornament Scroll

Bell Ornate

Bells Snowflake

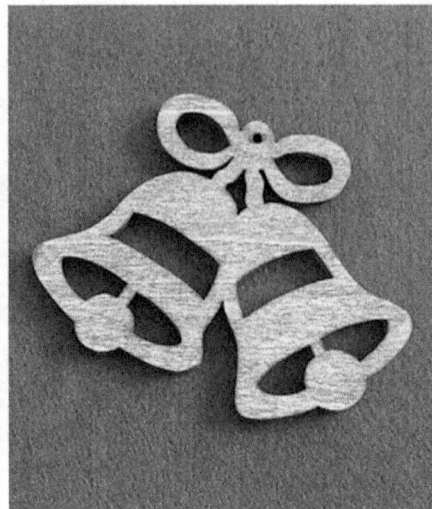

Bells Standard

Bow

*Calendar Holly*

*Candles*

*Candy Cane*

*Candy Cane with Bow*

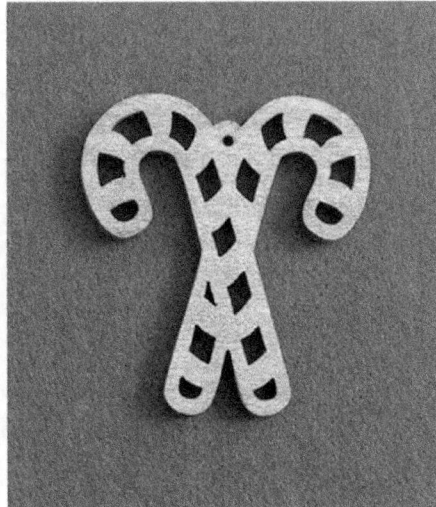

*Candy Canes Crossed*

*Carolers*

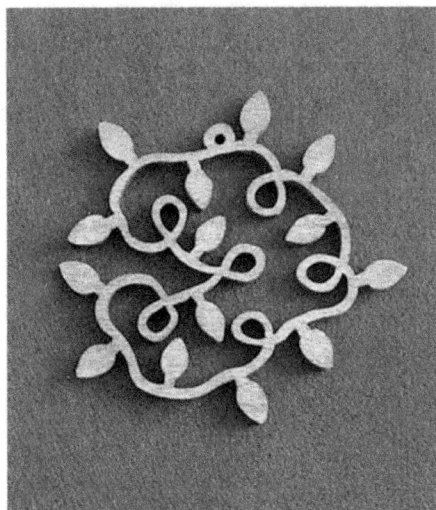

*Christmas Lights*

*Deer #1*

*Deer #2*

Deer Head

Elf #1

Elf #2

Elf #3

Gingerbread House Flowers

Gingerbread House Hearts

Gingerbread Man

Gingerbread Woman

Holly

*Mistletoe*

*Naughty List*

*Nice List*

*Nutcracker #1*

*Nutcracker #2*

*Nutcracker #3*

*Poinsettia*

*Present*

*Present Stack*

Sack of Presents

Santa Rooftop #1

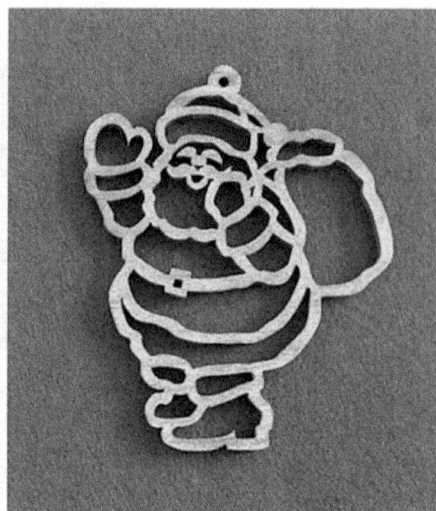

Santa with Pack

Star #1

Star #2

Stocking

Toy Soldier #1

Toy Soldier #2

Toy Soldier #3

Tree

Waiting For Santa Boy #1

Waiting For Santa Girl #1

Waiting For Santa Boy #2

Waiting For Santa Girl #2

Bass Clef

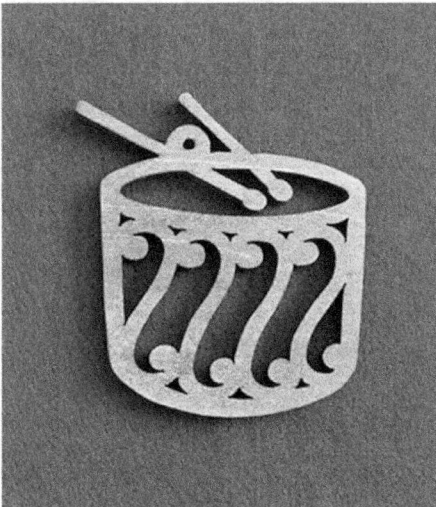

Drum

Eighth Note

Guitar

Handbell

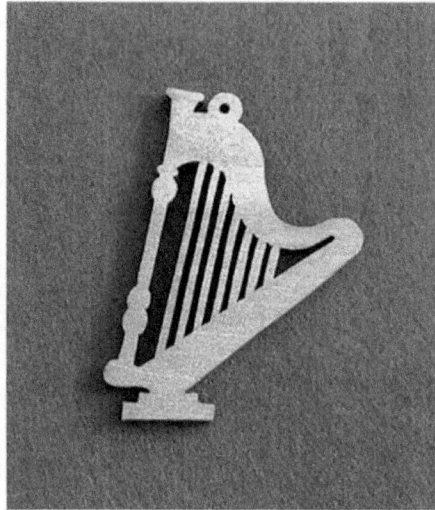

Harp

Horn with Bow

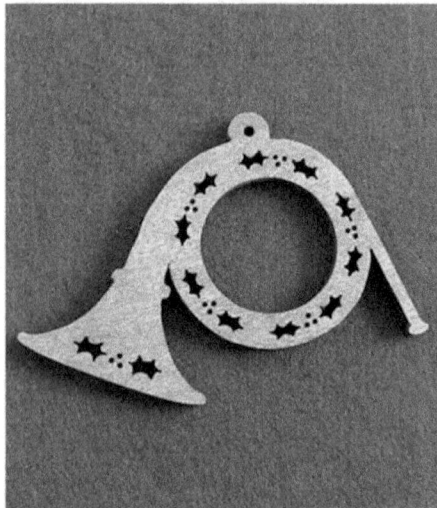

Horn with Holly

Lyre

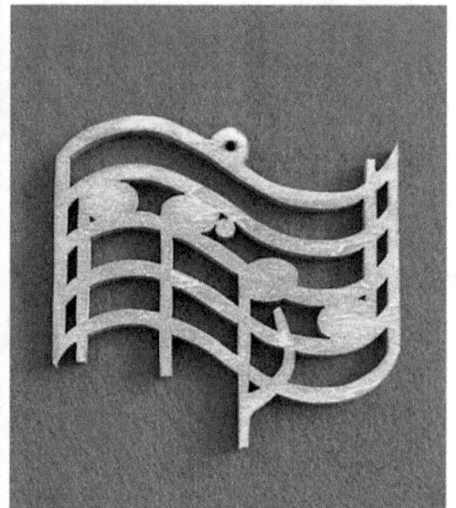

Music - Away In A Manger

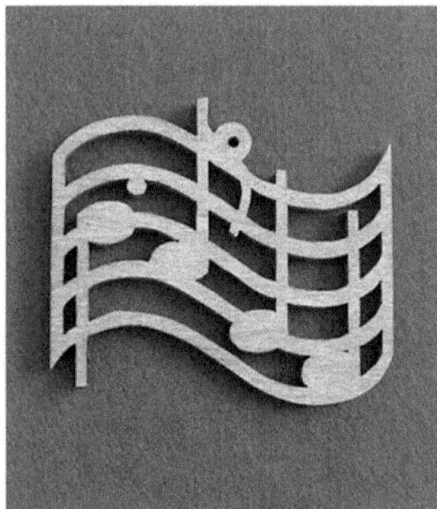

Music - Deck The Halls

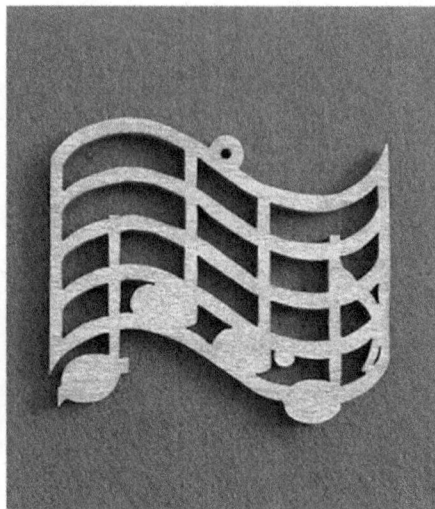

Music - Hark The Herald

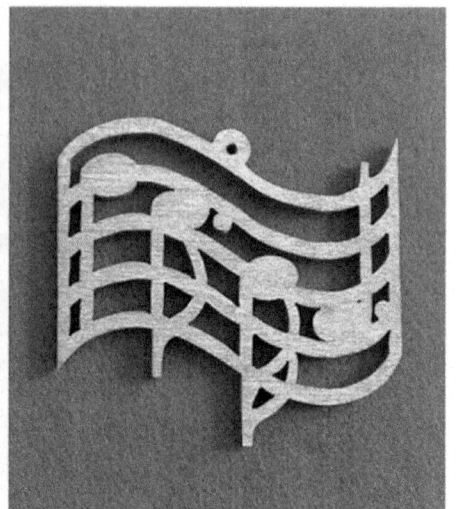

Music - Joy To The World

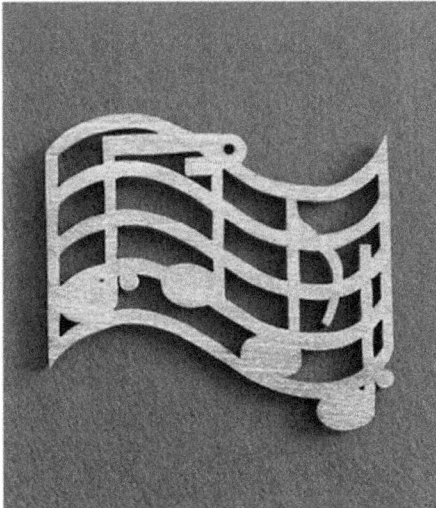

*Music - Slient Night*

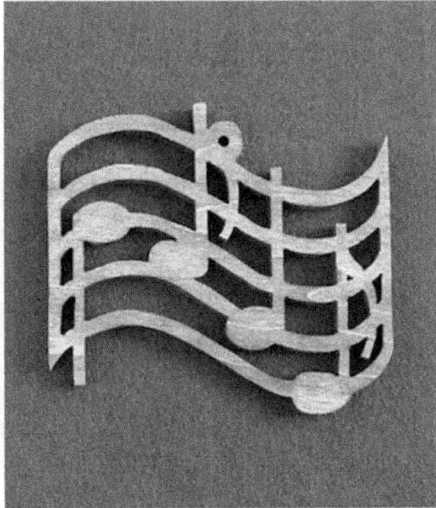

*Music - We Three Kings*

*Piano*

*Sixteenth Note*

*Treble Clef*

*Violin*

*Angel*

*Chi Rho*

*Choir Boy*

Choir Girl

Church #1

Church #2

Church #3

Church Window

Cross #1

Cross #3

Cross #4

Dove of Peace

Dove with Olive Branch

Holy Bible

ihs

Journey to Bethlehem

Luke 2:1-14

Manger

Wiseman

Baby Buggy

Baseball

Basketball

Blocks

Five of Clubs

Football

Jack In The Box Diamond

Jack In The Box Star

Picture Book E-F

Picture Book S-T

Pull Duck

Rag Doll Boy

Rag Doll Girl

Rattle - Flower

Rattle - Hearts

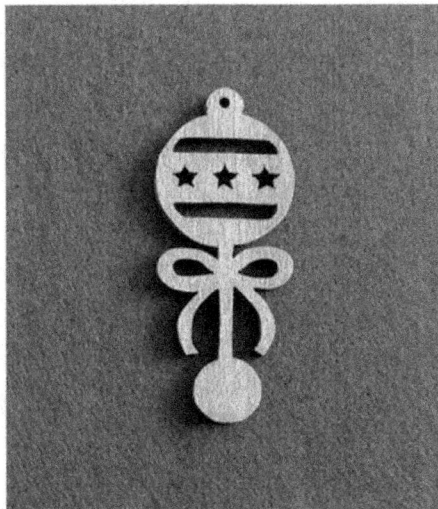

Rattle - Stars

Rocking Horse Western

Sail Boat

Soccer Ball

Teddy Bear Bow

Teddy Bear Heart

Train Engine

Tricycle Boy

Tricycle Girl

Believe

Blessings

Buon Natale

Celebrate

Deck The Halls

Faith

Family

Feliz Navidad

Good Will To Men

Happy Hanukkah

Happy Holidays

Happy New Year

Ho Ho Ho Holly

Ho Ho Ho Present

Hope

Jesus

Jesus Christ

Joy

Joyuex Noel

Let It Snow

Little Drummer Boy

Love

Make A Wish

Mary & Joseph

Merry Christmas

Mistletoe & Holly

Noel

North Pole

O Holy Night

Peace

Peace On Earth

Rejoice

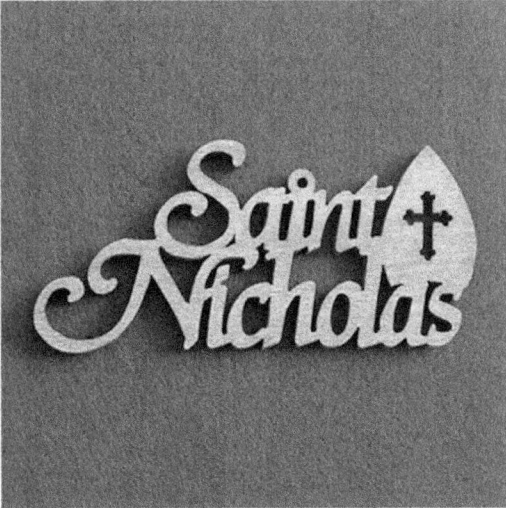

Saint Nicholas

Season's Greetings

Silent Night

Star Of Bethlehem

Think Snow

Winter Wonderland

Building A Snowman

Cardinal

Fireplace Stockings

Front Door #2

Ice Skater

Ice Skates

Lamp Post

Lantern

Mailbox

Mittens Crisscross

Mittens Snowflake

Mug Holly

Mug Snowflake

Skier

Sled

Sleigh

Snowman

Snowflake #1

Snowflake #2

Snowflake #4

*Snowflake #5*

*Snowflake #8*

*Snowflake #9*

*Snowflake #10*

*Snowflake #11*

*Snowflake #13*

*Snowflake #17*

*Snowflake #18*

*Snowflake #20*

# *Index*